CW00404348

ST KILDA SNAPSHOTS

based on

LACHLAN MACDONALD'S Collection

David A. Quine

The Islands Book Trust

Published in 2011 by The Islands Book Trust

www.theislandsbooktrust.com

ISBN: 978-1-907443-21-3

Text © David Quine

British Library Cataloguing in Publication Data. A CIP record for this book can be obtained from the British Library.

All rights reserved. No part of this publication may be reproduced, stored in a retrieval system, or transmitted in any other form or by any means, electronic, mechanical, photocopying, recording or otherwise without the prior written permission of the publishers. This book may not be lent, hired out, resold or otherwise disposed of by way of trade in any form of binding or cover other than that in which it is published, without the prior consent of the publishers.

The Islands Book Trust would like to thank Donnie Morrison for his help in the production of this book.

Cover images:
Front: Banner clouds over Boreray and the Stacs (© and courtesy of Jim Richardson/www.jimrichardsonphotography.com)
Back: Lachlan MacDonald at home in Glen Nevis with David Quine in 1989 (David A. Quine)

Typeset by Erica Schwarz (www.schwarz-editorial.co.uk)
Printed and bound by Martins the Printers, Berwick upon Tweed
Cover design by James Hutcheson

The Islands Book Trust,
Ravenspoint Centre, Kershader,
South Lochs, Isle of Lewis, HS2 9QA
Tel: 01851 880737

Contents

Acknowledgements

I am most grateful to the late Lachlan MacDonald and his wife, Nancy, for kindly giving me access and permission to reproduce their fascinating collection of photographs relating to life on St Kilda and after the evacuation which add a new dimension to the St Kilda story. I also appreciate the permission given to me to reproduce several old photographs now in the care of the National Trust for Scotland (NTS).

Nancy MacDonald receiving Honorary Membership of The Islands Book Trust from Alasdair MacEachen in August 2010

Acknowledgements for Photographs and Drawings

A – Robert Atkinson, NTS
AB – Arthur Barrington
C – Alex Cockburn, NTS
DAQ – David Quine
H – Norman Heathcote (drawing)
J – Robert Jobling (drawing)

LM – Lachlan MacDonald collection
M – Mrs M. MacDonald collection
MA – MacLeod, A.
MAA – MacGregor, A.A.
MM – R. C. MacLeod of MacLeod
NM – Norman MacLeod

NTS – National Trust for Scotland
O – E. Ogilvie collection
RC – Ronnie Cramond
W – Whyte, Inverness D

Illustrations

After the Evacuation – Lochaline District

THE ISLANDS BOOK TRUST – high quality books on island themes in English and Gaelic

Based in Lewis, the Islands Book Trust are a charity committed to furthering understanding and appreciation of the history of Scottish islands in their wider Celtic and Nordic context. We do this through publishing books, organising talks and conferences, visits, radio broadcasts, research and education on island themes. For details of membership of the Book Trust, which will keep you in touch with all our publications and other activities, see www.theislandsbooktrust.com or phone 01851 880737.

The Islands Book Trust, Ravenspoint, Kershader, South Lochs, Isle of Lewis, HS2 9QA (01851 880737)

Lachlan and Nancy MacDonald at their home in Glen Nevis in 1987

INTRODUCTION – MAGICAL ISLANDS

Fig. 1. Approaching St Kilda

My forebears lived on the Isle of Man, together with the Quiggins, Quillans and Kellys – islands seem to be in my blood. Over the years I have been able to visit the Pembrokeshire Islands of Skomer, Skokholm and Ramsey, then on to the Orkneys, Fair Isle and Shetland and many of the Hebrides – I also camped for three nights on the Bass Rock in the Firth of Forth where I could see the nests of a hundred gannets without getting out of bed!

In 1976 from North Uist I saw St Kilda, a tiny speck on the horizon, with its own banner cloud. Immediately I attempted to find a boat going there but I had to wait until the following year to fulfil my dream. St Kilda had been at the top of my list of islands to be visited since 1947 when I used to collect cuttings on birds and islands for my scrap-book. In *Country Life* I found an article by James Fisher of his visit to St Kilda with a wonderful photograph of the eastern cliffs of Hirta. This image of the island was filed away in the recesses of my mind as somewhere to visit in the future. Although it was 30 years before my dream was realised, I was overawed by the amazing numbers of nesting seabirds, the splendour and grandeur of the islands and, like every other visitor, I felt I must return.

Four St Kildans in 1977 at the St Kilda Club (DAQ)

In November of the same year I went to my first St Kilda Club meeting in Edinburgh. Immediately my wonder at the spectacular scenery was matched by my fascination at the absorbing human story of those who had lived there. Four people who had been born on St Kilda were present that day and I was thrilled to meet and photograph them. Neil Gillies, second from the left, who as a boy damaged his leg on St Kilda and had to go to hospital in Oban, then on to Glasgow from where his parents received the message that he was too ill to be operated on. But in due course he underwent an operation and lived on until he was 93 years old and died in 1990! The two ladies were Flora Craig, née Gillies, on the right and her cousin Rachel Johnston. The other was Lachlan MacDonald, on the left, from House No. 16, Main St, St Kilda whom I was going to get to know in the following years. In fact I have over ten hours of audio tape of Lachlan's memories of life on St Kilda, which I have deposited in the archives of the National Trust for Scotland.

Over the years Lachlan and his wife Nancy had been given photographs taken by visitors to St Kilda and had built these up into a collection of over sixty. They have kindly given me access to this and permission to publish them. Many are just snapshots, quite small – 2 × 3 inches (8 × 5 cm) – but all speak louder than words and form the basis of this book. I have added a few photographs from other sources.

1. LIFE ON ST KILDA

Mr Campbell and Nurse McKinlay

Life on St Kilda, 50 miles out into the Atlantic, has always been fraught with difficulties. The sea was looked on with fear, since many tragedies occurred; child-birth, infantile tetanus and other illnesses caused many deaths. Cliff-climbing for birds and their eggs had inherent dangers, and isolation during the winter often brought near starvation. The inhabitants benefited considerably from the assistance of resident ministers, teachers and the occasional nurse.

Mr Campbell and Nurse Ann McKinlay in 1884, with a group of St Kildans (W)

This early photo was taken in 1884 by D. Whyte from Inverness, and was rediscovered in Inverness in the 1980s by a lady who was wanting to exchange a painting in a frame. She removed the painting and was surprised to find this photograph as a support backing. Mr Campbell was the first of the schoolmasters to be sponsored by the Ladies' Association of the Highland Society of the Free Church.

A room in the Factor's House was made available for the teaching of English, geography, history, arithmetic and composition. Most of these teachers were young men and stayed for just one year. Connel (1887) commented:

> It hardly needs to be pointed out that the student who allows himself to be sent out to train the young St Kildian, even if only for a twelve month, does a heroic thing and is quite entitled to the gratitude of his church as the missionary who goes to Old Calibar or the Cannibal Islands.

Nurse Ann McKinlay, née MacLeod, came from Skye and married Murdoch McKinlay in Glasgow. Emily MacLeod, the sister of the Chief of the Clan on Skye, persuaded Ann to go to St Kilda as the first trained nurse on the island. She stayed from 1884 to 1886 in the Factor's House as a mid-wife and sorted out the care of newborn babies and managed to stop the terrible curse of infant lock-jaw. When she returned to Edinburgh in 1886 the St Kildans went back to their old ways and infantile tetanus quickly caused great distress again.

The Manse – Some of the Occupants

Fig. 2. The Kirk, School and Manse

There have been many remarkable people who have taken up residence in the Manse on St Kilda over the years. The following deserve fuller recognition:

The Rev. Neil MacKenzie – appointed to serve on St Kilda 1829–43:

Neil MacKenzie was born in Glen Sannox on Arran in 1795. After his theological training he offered to go to Labrador, but the place was taken by someone else so '*he volunteered to go to any place for which no-one else could be got, and it was this that eventually led to his being asked to go to St Kilda*' (MacKenzie, 1911). He was appointed to St Kilda on May 13th 1830, ordained on June 5th and arrived in St Kilda at 4 am on July 1st. He had been given an allowance for his journey by the SSPCK and some money to buy sheep on St Kilda. He was introduced to the people on the 1st and inducted on July 4th on the Sabbath by the Rev. Dr John MacDonald, the Apostle of the North, who had collected money for a new Kirk and manse on St Kilda. MacDonald described Neil as '*shy, unobtrusive, of retiring disposition. At first sight thought little in him, but with acquaintance discover him to be a man of mind and of good knowledge, a man of prudence, piety, firmness of principle and mildness of disposition, peculiarly fitting in the missionary of St Kilda.*' He had many gifts and had a great concern for the physical and spiritual needs of the people, nothing was too much trouble for him.

In 1834 Sir Thomas Dyke Acland, concerned for the welfare of the natives, gave Neil twenty sovereigns to encourage the inhabitants to destroy the miserable hovels in which they lived and build new houses. MacKenzie saw the need to plan out the new settlement and for the tacksman to arrange lots. The first attempt was rejected by the inhabitants and they, with MacKenzie's guidance, fixed the portions of the ground, drew lots and built a house on each plot. By 1838 twenty-one new houses were completed. The outcome of his work '*resulted in the appearance of an entirely new planned settlement*' (Macgregor, 1960). The Kirk and Manse had previously been erected in time for his actual arrival in 1830, when they were given their own triangular enclosure.

Between the Dry Burn and the Amhuinn Mhor the New Village was laid out in an open crescent, the houses regularly spaced, each with a field strip of about 25 m width stretching from the beach to the Head Dyke. The houses, now known as the 1834 houses, '*had their narrow end to the sea and were built on a standard plan with the byre, living area and sleeping quarters all under one roof. The byre was situated at the low side with a drain onto the cultivation plot.*'

When the houses were nearly completed in 1838 he recalled that '*it was necessary that I should go south to purchase with the money left by Sir Thomas (Dyke Acland) the windows and other things needed for their completion. I soon found that the money which I had was not nearly sufficient to purchase the things of which they stood in immediate need. I therefore went to Dr MacLeod of St Columba's, and some other kind friends, and they entered so heartily into the matter that in a short time I had a good supply of 21 glass windows, 21 tables, 47 bedsteads, 21 kitchen dressers, 21 chairs, 21 stools and crockery ready for shipment.*'

Neil's wife knew no Gaelic but occupied herself in teaching the management of children, the importance of proper cooking, sanitary matters, sewing to the girls and the virtues of soap and starch.

Neil wrote about many things of interest – the island traditions, thatching methods, the barley drying kiln, bird fowling and the arrival of the birds, their breeding cycles and their departures – he takes us through the year:

January – Our coasts continue to be dead, lonely and deserted. Soon they will receive their inhabitants. A gannet has been seen as soon as the 13th of this month. By the beginning of next month a good number of them will be on their accustomed rocks. Rooks and the black-hood crow are numerous. The latter are very troublesome, taking the thatch off houses, seeking for grain and insects which rest in the thatch. The want of fuel is very much felt. Every good day the natives are from hill to hill, and from crevice to cliff, in search of anything that burns.

February – The shearwater has come to these islands the latter end of this month. One third of all the gannets that arrive this year should now be about our rocks. The black guillemot having assumed the summer plumage is now seen. Our religious meetings have been regularly attended all the season. The scarcity of food and fuel, which is now felt in their intensity gives a sombre aspect to everything around us.

March – All the birds are now come except the puffin. Though the last in coming it is first generally that is now caught. Formerly the black and particularly the foolish guillemot used to be very early caught, but their mode of capture being more dangerous and certainly more laborious, they discontinued. All the birds are so regular in the time of leaving and coming, laying and hatching, that a kind of calendar might be constructed from their migrations. How well this illustrates the beautiful expression of Scripture,

Fig. 3. Head of Manx Shearwater

'Yea, the stork in the heavens knoweth her appointed times, and the turtle dove, and the crane, and the swallow, observe the time of their coming.'

April – All classes of sea-fowl are during this month about the island. About the end of it the puffin, gannet, shearwater and the black guillemot begin to lay. No fuel has been got yet; though it should be dry for a few days, there is not sufficient length of dry weather to dry turf. By the coming of the boat from Harris, and the arrival of the birds, the people's food is greatly improved. Every family got from forty to fifty gannets, besides small fowl. Thanks be to Almighty God for His kindness to us.

May – This is by far the most important season in the year to the fowler. All the birds lay in this month except the stormy petrel, which lays next month. The reason so many sea-fowl congregate upon our rocky island is to propagate their kind.

June – If deprived of the first laid eggs, that keeps them back two of three weeks, for they take sixteen days to lay a second. And a few – none of the fulmars lay a second egg – will not lay again at all. The people are ill off for fuel, they have got little, and still worst off for food.

July – All the birds are rearing their young, except the stormy petrel, during this month; but that little bird is only beginning to lay about the commencement of it. The people are suffering very much for want of food. During spring, ere the birds came, they literally cleared the shore not only of shell-fish but even of a species of sea-weed that grows abundantly on the rocks within the sea-mark. For a time they were better off particularly as long as fresh eggs could be got. Now the weather is coarse, birds cannot be found, at least in such abundance as their needs require. Sorrel boiled in water is their principal food and even the grass is getting scarce. All that was near is exhausted.

August – In the beginning of this month the guillemots and razorbills left their rocks, having got their young with them; the puffins about the 10th and also the kittiwakes; and towards the end the fulmars, having been robbed of its young.

St Kilda Field Mouse (DAQ)

September – The greater part of the gannets, with the old ones, leave our rocks about the end of this month. All birds leave our rocks as they get their young ones with them. The barley is not half shorn yet, nor the oats, this is decidedly the wettest and windiest season I remember. No fuel is got yet, neither is it likely that any will be this season. How the year is to be gone through I know not. Were it not for the promise that our bread would be given us and our water made sure, we should feel very uneasy.

October – The whole of the gannets are away from our rocks, and even the stormy- petrel. A few gulls, cormorants and black guillemots which turn greyish-white, remain about the shore all year. The fulmar continues coming to land every day the wind is from the west. A species of small duck visit the shores, and now and then an eider duck. When the weather is stormy, wild geese, and a few straggling swans, may be seen. Our crops are housed. The quantity of straw is large, but the grain very small. Potatoes are very defective, not above half an ordinary crop. No fuel has been got yet. Everything seems to conspire against us this season.

November – This is the deadliest month of the year. There is pleasure in seeing anything move in this more than solitary place. Our minds seem to be revived by seeing a few wildfowl such as swans, geese, woodcocks and snipes, though most of them pay us but a short visit on their way to more hospitable climes.

December – What has passed of this winter has been rather stormy. All kinds of fowls that come hither to breed are gone long ago to their winter quarters. Snipes, wrens, crows, ravens and hawks remain all the year round. Thrushes, lapwings, curlews, herons and ducks etc. visit us, and some of them remain with us for a long while in the winter. The people have never been worse off for fuel. Last year was not good, but this one turns out a third less.

'Lord have mercy upon us.'

When Dr James Wilson called at St Kilda in 1841 he was voyaging to acquire a general knowledge of fisheries of the whole coast of Scotland. He took Mackenzie on a trip out in his cutter, which included a night away from Hirta. Wilson commented: '*It need scarcely be said that we gave the minister the best cheer we had it in our power to bestow. He ate heartily of several unaccustomed articles and with undisguised and almost youthful relish which it was delightful to look upon. The curry-soup and pancakes were thought surprising, – the malt was swallowed, though deliberately, – the wine and liqueurs were almost entirely avoided. He said he had long led so abstemious a life from necessity.*'

After being entertained by a group of natives to show off their cliff climbing skills Neil MacKenzie was returned to St Kilda when the natives asked what the crew proposed to do with the minister, why had they kept him from home all night, and whether we had any intention of carrying him off to America, or any other foreign country? '*They added, that if we had the latter object in view, they hoped we would let them know in time, as they were all willing to accompany him wherever he might go!*' This was a high and heartfelt testimony of their affection.

On leaving St Kilda, the Rev. Neil MacKenzie served in the parish of Kilchrenan on the shores of Loch Awe, where a headstone marks his burial in 1878 aged 85 years and a plaque has been erected to his memory inside the Kirk.

Kilchrenan Church (DAQ)

Gravestone of the Rev. Neil MacKenzie (DAQ)

Rev. Angus Fiddes with a group of St Kildans (1890–1903)

It wasn't until the arrival of the Rev. Angus Fiddes that things improved regarding lock-jaw. He was on St Kilda from 1889 to 1903, the last of the ordained Free Church ministers. He soon became very concerned about the number of babies dying from infantile tetanus, as the women had reverted to their old ways of anointing the umbilical cord with fulmar oil and soil. He went to Glasgow to take a course on midwifery under Dr Turner, who recommended immediate and repeated application of iodoform to the stump of the umbilical cord until it had healed and the stump had come away. He returned to St Kilda to meet with stubborn resistance but gradually overcame the opposition. In the photograph he is on the right of the front row.

Alice MacLachlan with her new spinning wheel, St Kilda, 1906–09

Alice was the wife of the minister, Peter, sent to St Kilda in 1906. He had studied law at Glasgow University, then at Edinburgh before he became a missionary. Alice was born in Haddington and became a qualified teacher. She was known to have kept diaries during her stay on the island. As I was unable to track these diaries down I asked at a St Kilda Club meeting if anyone could help me – sadly no-one had seen them. However, it alerted one of the NTS staff who, delving into the archives for information on the feather-store, pulled out an envelope, when unexpectedly a second one fell onto the floor – '*Typescript of the diaries of Alice MacLachlan*'. What a treasure trove! In the meantime I had managed to make contact with her daughter, Susan, then a nurse in a clinic in Harare, Zimbabwe. She informed me that she was coming to England and would send me the original three volumes. What a thrill it was to handle such wonderful documents.

Alice knew no Gaelic but kept a wonderful diary detailing the everyday events throughout the year. She included the name of every boat that called, often naming the skippers, every accident that occurred as well as the changing weather patterns. She even gave birth to her baby, Susan, on the island. She delighted in her new spinning wheel obtained through the factor, Mr McKenzie, '*it is a beauty, made of teak wood.*' (Fri May 8th 1908.)

On May 12th 1908 she commented that '*men sometimes went to Scalpay to try to find a wife.*'

On Sept 23rd, '*A man and his wife from Harris and the wife's sister also came as guests of Hugh Gillies' House (to spy out the land and see if the sister would stay as Hugh's wife) – the girl was not willin!*'

Sept 24th – '*Great excitement tonight. A tug, the Oceana (Capt. Pickard) came in. They were looking for a grain elevator which they had lost near Tory Island, NW Ireland. It had drifted away up north and they called here on their way outwards. The captain and crew were all Irishmen.*'

Sept 25th – '*We heard with great amusement that the women of the village all congregated in one or two houses last night expecting the wild Irishmen from the tug would come ashore and murder them. They consoled themselves that the enemy would begin at the Manse, and they would hear shrieks up there and they could flee! The boat left early and the women went to bed!!! The elevator was found three days later and taken to Stornoway!*'

Many of the trawler skippers were extremely helpful in visiting shops on behalf of the St Kildans as shown in the entry for Mon 18th Feb 1907:

The 'Knowsie', Aberdeen, came round the Point of Coll. He only left here at mid-day on Wednesday and returned in two days less than a week and brought back all the things ordered. The men bungled their order and instead of bringing some small pieces of cheese he brought two huge cheeses – one of 84lbs and another of 96lbs at 10d per lb. The people wanted us to take them, but what could we do with so much. Besides we ordered some from Fleetwood and so did most of the people and some got their order yesterday!

On March 22nd 1909, Alice records the tragic drowning of Donald MacDonald and Norman and John MacQuien. She reveals the desperate situation as it unfolds. It is the only account and is included in full:

Glorious, I am still in bed (expecting the birth of my baby). Think of getting up later in the day. Just like summer and so warm. Two boats left about 10 or a little after for Boreray to see about sheep etc. and Kate told me when she came to tidy my room that five men, Donald MacDonald, John Gillies, Neil MacKinnon, Norman McQuien and his brother John, went to Dun in William's boat. Kate had gone out of the room and my window was left wide open as the day was so lovely. All at once I heard the most terrible cries from the Dun and I called to Kate who ran out, and in turn gave the alarm up that something had happened at the Dun. Dunie came from school in time to help old Angus, Finlay Mor and Finlay McQuien, and in a very short time they got over to the scene of whatever happened. The suspense at home was awful, the women were all down and anguished weeping and wailing, I cannot describe. However, the boat came, and our worst fears were realised; worse than we ever imagined. Donald MacDonald, Norman and John McQuien were all drowned. Neil McKinnon and John Gillies were rescued in a very exhausted condition. Donald MacDonald's body was found floating in the water but poor Norman and John had gone down gripping each other. The scenes were indescribable. Dunie up twice. A beacon was lighted at Berenahake to make the men come home as it seemed they proposed staying to kill gannets. Poor Donald Og and Ewen McDonald.

Wed 24th March – *Donald McDonald was buried today. Most terribly sad.*

Thurs 25th March – *Great many visitors myself these days as I am not at all well, though better. No boats.*

Fri 26th March – *This week is like a month. The bodies have not been recovered. Dunie and Kate up. I was out a wee bit in the sun today, with my big coat on.*

Sat 27th March – *Out a good while today. Rachel Ferguson very low today. People as sad as ever.*

Sun 28th March – *My birthday. Up most of the day. Capt. Walckner arrived during the day and was terribly shocked at the news. Went and trawled for the bodies but no signs. Brought me my medicine and a box of ointment from himself. He had the poorest trip he ever made, only £47. He is wanted to go to Iceland. Services in church terribly pathetic today. I was not allowed to go out.*

Mon 29th March – *Got letters today. People a wee bit braver today. Poor things. It is awfully sad, especially for Beau Toromich. Hens doing fairly well. Very stormy day today and yesterday. The young factor says Miss Kemble is coming for a fortnight to study the birds.*

Sun Apr. 4th – *Donald og and the three McDonald boys were at church though I am still a prisoner. Torrents of rain and very high wind.*

Fig. 4. Trawler with Oiseval behind

Mrs Cameron and her two daughters (right) on St Kilda

The Rev. Donald Cameron was a lay missionary of the United Free Church of Scotland, a native of Ballachulish in Argyll, his wife came from North Uist and was a renowned good cook and teacher. They stayed for seven years although the normal course was three. They loved the island, and the people; they were loathe to leave when the time came. One of their daughters wrote her memoirs of the time on the island. She comments that her '*mother was horrified that there were no fences round the cliffs. Wind and storms – even in the summer – one left us deaf for a week – there were 47 trawlers in the bay for the night. We were 11 weeks without mails – we were opening Christmas cards in March. We read in the paper that due to a strike people in London had to go without their morning papers for three days! We had never heard such hearty singing anywhere as in Church in St Kilda. School inspection was after midnight on Sunday. Whooping cough and mumps went right through the village and influenza in 1926 (which came from a trawler-man) when four of the older men died in a week – a crippling blow to a small community.*'

Lachlan MacDonald commented in 1986, '*I remember the Camerons well. He was always keen to get something into your head. He started holding meetings in the evenings twice a week. I went with my sister Cathy for a few weeks, but we soon dropped out.*'

John MacLeod and the School in 1927 (C)

Back row: Missionary and Schoolmaster John MacLeod, Finlay MacKinnon and Donald Ewen MacKinnon.

Middle row: Donald Gillies, Cathie Gillies, Flora Gillies, Mary Ann Gillies, Rachel MacKinnon and Alick MacLeod (son of the Missionary).

Front row: Ewen Gillies and Kenneth MacLeod (younger son of Mr MacLeod). Sometimes the older men also attended school.

Alick MacLeod in 1979 (DAQ)

I first met John's son Alick in 1979. He was camping on St Kilda; I was about to take a service in the kirk when a man passed the doorway of the cottage, I told him my intention and if he cared to join us we would be very pleased. I explained to him that to reach the kirk you went down the path, turned right past the bell… He quietly interrupted me and said, '*I do know the way, I used to live here!*' So began a great and valued friendship as he had become the teacher of Gaelic in the school at Tarbert in Harris. With his knowledge of St Kilda and the Gaelic I pestered him with all my Gaelic queries. He was always invaluable and scholarly in his replies.

Alick's first impressions of St Kilda as a boy were the '*incredible lushness of the Manse Glebe grass – a veritable jungle of knee-high growth, also on a winter's night seeing Village Bay fully illuminated with the lights of the Fleetwood trawlers sheltering from a storm. My clearest and fondest memory of Sunday School is the period when it was conducted by the geologist, Alick Cockburn – in English, of course, as Mr. Cockburn had no Gaelic. He was a delightful young man, very devout and we worshipped him, He was equally popular with the adults.*

In school one day a boy was asked what he wanted, in reply, he thought he was saying, "I am thirsty." What in fact he said was, "I am drunk!" He got his Gaelic idiom somewhat out of focus. It made our day! One time a minister came to take our communion service, but the weather broke and he was stranded for a while on the island. Eventually he escaped on a whaler heading back to Harris!

Alick's father, John MacLeod, was the lay-missionary on St Kilda from 1926 to 1929. He was born in 1885 in Berneray in the Sound of Harris, where he worked with his father as a lobster fisherman in the dangerous nearby waters. He later obtained his First Mate ticket and served as a steward in ships and yachts around the world. He married in 1912 and during the war served in the 2/4 Cameron Highlanders and returned to ships soon after. Gaelic was spoken at home and he developed a deeper interest in Christian doctrine and theology. Sadly his wife died and the three children returned to Berneray to be looked after by close relatives and John returned to the sea.

In 1924 John remarried a widow, Elizabeth Gamble. John had many gifts including a good tenor voice; he led the singing in the Gaelic Services, taught himself the bagpipes, enjoyed watercolour painting and became a lay-missionary in the United Free Church:

On St Kilda he was thrown in at the deep end as he was Head of the school and responsible for the spiritual oversight of the island. On Sunday morning the service was in Gaelic with an English resume, the evening service was entirely in Gaelic. The inhabitants could pray quite spontaneously, remarkable for the elegance and facility of the language and the depth of spiritual language shown. One irritant was that one of the congregation had a pocket watch which he checked regularly and closed with a loud 'click' which reverberated round the church. Visiting was no problem to John, it was a labour of love.

Alick commented:

The trawlers, mainly from Fleetwood, sheltered in Village Bay. How indebted we were to those intrepid mariners. They ferried our mails to and fro, they gave us generous gifts of fish and they gave us their time and company by coming ashore and visiting our houses. One other memory is that of listening to broadcast services on the radio, or 'wireless' as we used to call it. Apart from the weather forecast and the news my father was not much addicted to it.

If the St Kildans were poor materially, they were abundantly rich in the moral and spiritual virtues that constitute real wealth. Wresting as they did a living from their environment, they were rich in their knowledge and understanding, and appreciation of their environment. They were rich in Christian faith and were rich in the graces that stem from that faith. Thus they lived together in unity, and their differences were of a minor nature incidental to living in such close proximity to each other. They were open and honest, mutually helpful, and generous to a degree, as we in the Manse were privileged to know. They were affectionate by nature and quickly endeared themselves to all those with whom they came in contact.

After leaving St Kilda the family went to Staffin on Skye, father serving as a missionary (or lay-preacher). In 1934 he was sent to Lochaline in Morven where he was re-united with many of his former St Kilda congregation, some of them were by now settled in Lochaline itself and some were at Larachbeg and Savary a few miles from Lochaline.

St Kilda Parliament in 1886 (NM)

Alastair Alpin MacGregor commented: '*Neighbouring Boreray was the limit of their foreign policy; and even then, that policy was concerned solely with sheep, with sea-birds and their eggs.*' Alexander Carmichael commented: '*The rules of the council are as inelastic as brass. Woe betide the crofter who would propose an iota of change on the ways of the fathers. All are allowed to attend, but only house-holders to speak.*'

In the photograph the smaller man, third on the left, is Donald MacDonald of House 16, the father of Lachlan MacDonald. On the right, the first man is Donald Ferguson, the Ground Officer, and next to him is 'Red' Gillies (John Gillies), the only man on St Kilda with a red beard, who died of influenza before the evacuation. He was from House 15.

Gannet nesting ledge on Boreray (DAQ)

Fig. 5. The Kyle of Dun

Alex Cockburn and Nurse Littlejohn

Alex Cockburn and Nurse Littlejohn, 1927 (MA)

Cockburn was 25 when he arrived on St Kilda to assist Mathieson in the surveying of St Kilda. Mathieson had been a geographer and cartographer based at Edinburgh University and had been on Scott's Antarctic Expedition earlier and on a trip to Spitsbergen in 1926. They produced the first detailed map of St Kilda, six inches to the mile.

Cockburn had obtained a first class honours degree in Geology at Edinburgh and went on to study the volcanoes of Hawaii and the Coast Ranges of Columbia. He wrote the *Geology of St Kilda* which was published in 1935 in the *Transactions of the Royal Society of Edinburgh*. He became Senior Lecturer and Director of Studies at Edinburgh University. He was also an excellent photographer.

Cockburn chose Ewen MacDonald to descend the cliffs and obtain geological samples for him. He was so impressed by his skills that he named his own son Ewen after him.

Nurse Littlejohn is photographed outside the Factor's House in 1927. She served on St Kilda from 1925 until early 1928 when she was taken ill and was replaced by Nurse Barclay.

St Kilda Parliament

St Kilda Parliament in 1927 (C)

Left to right: Ewen Gillies, Norman MacKinnon (senior), John Gillies, Ewen MacDonald (above the head of Ewen Gillies), Donald Gillies (standing), Neil Ferguson (junior, sitting), Finlay MacKinnon (sitting), Neil Gillies (standing, died in 1928), Lachlan MacDonald, Donald MacDonald, Norman MacKinnon (junior), Finlay Gillies, Neil Ferguson (senior), Donald Ewen MacKinnon, Malcolm (Blind Calum) MacDonald.

Fig. 6. The Stacs and Boreray from the Gap

Lachlan MacDonald recalled his experience:

They would suggest what they were going to do – if they were going out in a boat, or going to the rocks or they might decide to 'divide the rocks' – they did it by lots. The cliffs were shared for the grass and for the birds – you all had a good lot of little bits all round the island. It was the same if you were killing fulmars and you were counting them and putting them into heaps, you would still cast lots so that it would be even and no-one could say that those birds were better because they were in that lot. The same was if you were with the fish. You cast lots. It was great – so there would be no argument! Everything was done so that all worked together. Sometimes we discussed for a long time and sometimes no. When it got heated up, you would stand up, walk around, shake your arms, walk off in a 'huff' and come back again.

2. THE LAST INHABITANTS

Along the Village Street – Houses 1–16

Along the Village Street, Houses 1–16 (DAQ)

Several factors led to the eventual evacuation of the islands in 1930. In 1852 half of the 36 islanders emigrating to Australia on the *Priscilla* sadly died on the voyage or in quarantine within weeks of landing. They had no immunity to the diseases to which they were exposed. Their departure was a loss from which the St Kilda community was never able to recover. Their number was reduced from 110 in 1830 to 73 in 1856 with the loss of many of the young men required for the strenuous manual work on the agricultural plots and with the skills for climbing the cliffs.

During the First World War a small naval detachment was based on St Kilda and many of the ratings came from Glasgow and talked of an easier way of life in the city. When the war was over several of the young St Kildans left to find a new life.

Fig. 7. Doorway of Rachel MacCrimmon's house

In 1926 an outbreak of influenza caused the deaths of four of the senior men and in 1929–30 two of the younger women lost their lives to TB and appendicitis. This broke the spirit of the remaining inhabitants. With the help of the missionary and the nurse they requested the Government that arrangements should be made for everyone to leave the island before the next winter. On August 30th 1930 the people left on *HMS Harebell*; the sheep and cattle had been taken off on the previous day on the *Dunara Castle*.

House No. 1 – MacKinnon Family – Norman (see 1927 St Kilda Parliament)

Norman was the Precentor at the church services and was considered to be the most skilful tailor on the island, a gift which would help to clothe the eight children in the family. In the photograph his wife Annie MacKinnon and Finlay struggle their way up Conachair with the fulmars, caught by the men on the steep cliff. They are taking them back to the village for plucking.

Norman and his wife Annie, a daughter of Finlay Gillies of No. 7, were extremely short of food in the winter of 1929–30 and decided they would have to leave before the next winter.

Two St Kilda Friends (LM)

Left: Mrs Annie MacKinnon, the mother of 8 children. *Right*: Mrs Cathie Gillies married Neil Gillies – she was sister of Lachlan MacDonald. Both were very good neighbours on St Kilda. Neil sadly died in December 1928.

Mrs MacKinnon and her son Finlay bring fulmars home from Conachair (C)

Donald Ewen MacKinnon – pretending to be the captain of the ship! (LM)

Rachel MacKinnon as a little girl (LM)

House No. 2 – Finlay MacQueen

Finlay MacQueen was the inspiration for Norman Heathcote's sketch of landing on Stac Lee. A metal peg had previously been driven into the rock, a rope was thrown over it, and in bare feet, when the boat was on the rise, Finlay stepped out onto the rock. One of the wardens, Wally Wright, surprised me by saying that it was easier to land on Stac Lee (than Stac an Armin) because it is vertical!

Finlay MacQueen, St Kilda cragsman (A)

Finlay accompanied the Keartons on every expedition they undertook, also Norman Heathcote in 1898 and 1899. Oliver Pike, the early cine photographer, said of the St Kildans, '*They were absolutely fearless on the cliffs and are the finest climbers to be seen in the world*'.

Landing on Stac Lee (H)

Fig. 8. Stac Lee from Boreray

Like all the St Kildans, Finlay was skilful in using their long rods for catching the birds, especially puffins. At the end of the rod was a sliding noose or several which was laid flat on the ground. The puffin would step into the noose which would tighten and the bird would be caught. Sometimes 600 could be caught in a day.

In 1884 Finlay married Mary Jemima Otter Gillies. She had been born in 1860; the year when Captain Henry C. Otter of *HMS Porcupine*, the Government Survey Vessel, was caught in a severe October storm which tore the roofs off several houses, leaving only two still with their thatch, destroyed the only St Kildan boat and blew crops into the sea. The *Porcupine* was badly damaged and very nearly wrecked on the rocks. The Captain gave the inhabitants meal and a barrel of biscuits from the ship's supplies and small sails to protect the sick until their houses could be re-thatched. One month later the Captain returned with renewed supplies for the St Kildans. He also agitated for better housing and made a start on clearing rocks for the pier. In May 1860 his wife, Jemima Otter, who had been on board the *Porcupine*, came on land to assist in the delivery of Mary Gillies who was given this unusual name of Jemima Otter.

Finlay was very proud of the bird specimens that he had stuffed and loved to have his photograph taken of his puffin and gannet! Two of his brothers, Norman and John, were drowned in the dreadful accident off Dun in 1909 when Donald MacDonald met the same end. Finlay and his wife had a daughter, Mary Annie, who married Neil Ferguson junior, in the last wedding on St Kilda. Another daughter, Annie, married Donald Gillies of House No. 13 and a third, Christine, married John MacDonald, who died in a fall from the rocks with Ewen Gillies in 1916. They had two other daughters, Bessie and Christine, and another son Donald.

House No. 3 – MacDonalds

Three generations of MacDonalds from House No. 3, empty before the evacuation (MM)

Fig. 9. Stac an Armin

The MacDonalds had been on St Kilda since 1753, when they helped to repopulate the islands after the terrible smallpox outbreak of 1727–28. Three men and eight boys had been landed on Stac an Armin in August expecting to stay for 10 days to collect feathers and the young solan geese. During this time the epidemic broke out on Hirta. A St Kildan had died of the disease whilst in Harris and someone had thoughtfully returned his clothes, not anticipating the possible consequences – the awful outbreak on St Kilda. The epidemic caused 94 deaths, leaving only 4 adults and 26 children from 21 families. It struck so quickly that a crew could not be raised to man a boat to collect the party on the rock. They had to remain there until the Factor came in the middle of next May. They were all surprisingly well, '*They had lived on fish and fowls, but at times had suffered from cold and hunger. They made fish-hooks out of a few rusty nails, and also contrived to stitch together their clothing with feathers and patch them with the skins of birds. They returned mostly to empty houses, crops generally never reaped, and the cattle roaming about half wild.*' (Mackenzie, 1904.)

On another occasion, due to the boat smashing up on the rocks on Hirta, a group of men were marooned on Boreray throughout the winter. When they were rescued they were described as well '*but much out of humour*'!

William MacDonald suffered badly from asthma and in 1924 the whole family left, the first family to leave Hirta, which was a tremendous blow to the community. They moved to Stornoway on the Island of Lewis. In the photograph on p. 33 the rolls of cloth have been piled up ready for export and show (left to right) Grandfather Neil MacDonald, his son William, an unknown visitor, Finlay MacQueen and the boy in the centre is Calum MacDonald.

Calum served Lord Dumfries for four years before amazingly ending up as valet in the Grosvenor House Hotel, Park Lane, London for 26 years. He wrote an account of his time there and the people he met including Billy Graham, Doris Day, Rock Hudson, His Highness the Sultan of Brunei, George Formby, Sir Oswald Mosely, Sir Gerald Nabarro, Enoch Powell and the racing driver, Jackie Stewart. A far cry from St Kilda!

MacDonalds from No. 3 in front of the Factor's House (M)

The two boys are (left) Calum with Finlay John against the wall – seated Mrs MacKinnon.

Calum MacDonald (on left) after leaving St Kilda. He was Footman, later Valet (1936), to Lord Dumfries (M)

John MacDonald and sister May after their evacuation (LM)

This was taken before the main evacuation but after the MacDonalds had already moved to the island of Lewis.

House No. 4 – Empty at the Evacuation

This had been the house of Donald Ferguson (seen in the 1886 photo of the St Kilda Parliament). He was the Ground Officer whose son Alex left early for Glasgow where he became a successful cloth merchant and kept his close links with the St Kildans, helping them out on many occasions and visiting the islands regularly.

House No. 4 in a dilapidated state following the evacuation. The Post Office extension can be seen against neighbouring House No. 5 (Roger Anthony Bagnall Collection/NTS)

House No. 5 – The Fergusons

Donald's son Neil became the Postmaster and another son Donald was ordained. The photo shows the skipper of a visiting yacht, Neil Ferguson senior, Donald Gillies, Lachlan MacDonald and the boy, Donald MacKinnon, Lachlan's nephew. Outside No. 5 were the seats where the Parliament was held. The Fergusons were always in charge of these; meeting at about 10 am they would discuss ideas for the day, often until lunch time, '*If they were going anywhere desperate they would shout around and say they were going to Soa or Boyra.*'

Mrs Annie Ferguson on the Main Street on a windy day (LM)

Neil had married the half sister of Finlay MacQueen, here seen in the village with the washing line outstretched. She did not like having her photograph taken.

Neil Ferguson and others at the Pier (LM)

Fig. 10. Head of Gannet

Alex Ferguson visits from Glasgow. Helping the boys to blow birds eggs for sale (O)

Lachlan described going to the stacs in early May for gannets' eggs:

> *We would just visit for the day and be back at night. We would land, a couple of us would work together. We had a rope between us and one would go for maybe 50–60 yards or so and the other fellow would come up to there, and we would work it in bits like that right up to the top. You had an empty box on your back and when you got to the top you would start filling up the box with eggs, mostly gannets' eggs, you might get the odd guillemot egg but no many of them. There might be half a dozen of us, and you would work your way down and you would fill up the boxes as you were coming down. You would get it on your back then and you would carry it down. When you came near the place we would lower them with a rope into the boat. These boxes when full would be anything up to about a half to one cwt, an awful lot of eggs. You would get a wee bit of the nest and put it in the box before putting the lid on to stop them breaking. It was wonderful how they weren't broken – sometimes one or two would be. Then we would take them home. When you got home you would make a hole in the eggs and blow them and sell them to the visitors. What you blew out you could eat as well – they were great for making pancakes and things like that. If you couldn't eat it all you could give it to your beasts.*

Ferguson Brothers, the Rev. Donald and Alex; sons of Donald (O)

Alex was the first son and left the island in 1892 aged 19 and worked in Coopers Store in Glasgow before becoming a very successful tweed merchant selling his wares in London and Norway. He had a great love for the St Kildans and his native isle. He owned his own boat and made frequent visits to and from St Kilda. He took away dried fish and St Kilda tweed for sale in the city; provisions and people were passing both ways.

Donald was the youngest of the family, being born in 1880, and left St Kilda soon after his brother Alex in about 1896 to serve his apprenticeship with Yarrow Co., the shipbuilders on the Clyde, where he qualified as a ship's carpenter. He founded the Highland Mission in Partick, Glasgow, where he had a congregation of five hundred. He then trained for the ministry at Edinburgh University and the Free Church College. He married and had six children. He was very fond of the sea and bought a lifeboat and converted it into a cruiser with six berths. He went on many holidays up to Tobermory where he could visit Lochaline and link up with the St Kildans.

House No. 6 – Empty

Angus Gillies and his wife Annie had died well before the evacuation.

Angus and Annie Gillies lost six of their seven children in infancy.
The surviving son Finlay died tragically in 1898 aged 20 and his
memorial stone in the cemetery is shown above (Ian McHardy/NTS)

House No. 7 – Finlay Gillies

Finlay Gillies was often seen fowling for puffins with his rope with the sliding noose on the end. At the time of the evacuation Finlay was the oldest inhabitant, being in his 74th year. He was a good man, liked by all.

Three generations of Gillies (C)

On the left is Finlay, whose wife Catherine had died earlier; on the right is his son Neil who had married Lachlan MacDonald's sister Cathie; in the middle is the younger of Neil's sons, Ewen (the other being Donald). Neil is in the 1927 photo of the Parliament but was soon to fall ill and had to go to hospital in Oban, where he died in December 1928. After that Finlay lived with Cathie, along with the two boys Donald and Ewen born in 1918 and 1921 and Granny Gillies.

Cathie Gillies and sons; Donald, the elder, and Ewen (LM)

When Neil died in Oban hospital there was no way that Cathie could get off the island. Alex Ferguson made the funeral arrangements and Neil was buried in the cemetery at Pennyfuir, near Oban. Cathie's brothers Angus and Donald MacDonald were living in Glasgow at the time and were able to attend the funeral.

End of the Village – Gillies Empire (Seven houses had belonged to Gillies families)

*The far end of the Village
(DAQ)*

Fig. 11. Dun from Conachair

House No. 8 – Empty

This had been the home of 'Old Blind Calum' (see 1927 Parliament) who had died before the evacuation. He would preach in the absence of the Missionary and the Elder. He had married twice, first to Kirsty Gillies and then to Annie Gillies, the daughter of Norman Gillies and the sister of Finlay. His son Donald and daughter Annie had both left before the evacuation.

Mary MacLean (née MacDonald) and her son
Calum back on St Kilda at House No. 8
(Tom MacLean/NTS)

House No. 9 – J. R. MacDonald and Annie Gillies

J. R. MacDonald, brother of William, had left St Kilda from House No. 3 in 1924, but had the urge to return. Also living in No. 9 was Annie Gillies, known as Mrs Scalpay Gillies, whose husband had died from a fall from the rocks beyond Mullach Mor with Ewen MacDonald in August 1916. Also in the house was Annie's daughter Mary Anne. Some of the men went to the island of Scalpay to try to obtain a wife (see MacLachlan diary May 1908).

How the village looked about the time of the evacuation (Chris Mylne/NTS)

House No. 10 – Empty

Norman MacQueen had moved to Glasgow. He and his brother John were drowned off Dun in 1909.

Fig. 12. Ruins of the blackhouse of Malcolm MacQueen, a relative who emigrated to Australia in 1852

House No. 11 – Mrs Christine (Kirsty) MacQueen

Mrs MacQueen, née MacKinnon, lived here alone after her husband Norman and his brother John MacQueen were drowned off Dun in the terrible accident with Donald MacDonald in 1909. She was the aunt of Norman MacKinnon and had no children.

A view from Hirta of Dun, where the tragic drowning accident happened in 1909 (RC)

House No. 12 – Empty

Ewen Gillies had lived in this house until his fall from the rocks, when his widow Annie and daughter Mary Anne moved to No. 9.

Fig. 13. Before Ewen Gillies, this croft was occupied by Finlay MacQueen who was one of 36 St Kildans who emigrated to Australia in 1852. His daughter Rachel was one of those who died on the voyage. The ship on which the St Kildan emigrants sailed was the Priscilla, *which left from Birkenhead where this sketch of the Government Emigrant Depot was made. (Illustrated London News, 10 July 1852)*

House No. 13 – Gillies

Puffin noose (DAQ)

This puffin noose was given by Donald Gillies to John Gladstone, botanist, on his visit to St Kilda in the summer of 1927. He described Donald as *'a kind simple man who has inherited all the old St Kilda virtues. He has a family, he proudly told me of two girls, three dogs, two white cats without tails, one hen and chickens and one wife!'*

Donald Gillies with his pails of water (LM)

Rachel and Cathy Gillies after the evacuation (LM)

Fig. 14. Puffin in flight

Rachel, left, is one of two St Kildans living at the time of publication and is in the 1977 St Kilda Club photo. Cathy was three and a half years older and died a few years ago. Both parents, Donald and Christine, née Gillies, died in the same year, 1974. (Donald was the brother of the Rev. Donald John Gillies and of Neil, who had the bad leg, both of No. 15).

House No. 14 – Mrs Annie Gillies

Mrs Annie Gillies, née MacQueen, lived here with her daughters after her husband died of appendicitis whilst attending the sheep on Boreray in June 1922. She lived with her two daughters: Rachel, who married Mr Milne, and Flora, who married Mr Craig. Flora is in the 1977 St Kilda Club photo. They had two sisters who died, Kirsty of mumps aged 12 in 1925 and Mary of TB in July 1930.

Boreray and its Stacs (RC)

House No. 15 – John Gillies and Annie Ferguson

The Bride and Bridegroom, John Gillies and Annie Ferguson (J)

This sketch of John and Annie was drawn just before their wedding in 1890 by a professional artist, Robert Jobling, visiting St Kilda from Newcastle upon Tyne. He was a skilled artist and sketched the St Kildans bird fowling on the cliffs. He had shown considerable talent when he was only six years old '*depicting the scenes and subjects in the immediate neighbourhood of his home on the Tyne. He spent all his spare hours drawing and painting.*'

John Gillies was the 'Red' Gillies in the 1886 photo of the Parliament. He was the son of Donald Gillies and Margaret MacCrimmon and he died in the dreadful influenza outbreak in 1926. The bride was Annie Ferguson, the daughter of Donald Ferguson (seen in the 1886 Parliament photo). They produced a remarkable family of five sons: Donald, b. 1891, later married Christine MacKinnon and had two girls Rachel and Catherine living at No. 13. Donald died aged 83.

Norman John Gillies and his parents, John and Mary (née MacQueen) in 1925 (LM)

John Gillies as a child (NTS)

John, b. 1893; seen here as a child ringing the school bell. In the next photograph he is seen with his wife Mary (née MacQueen) in 1925 with their baby son Norman John, named after Mary's two brothers who were drowned with Donald MacDonald in 1909. Mary sadly died of appendicitis in February 1930 and John died when he was 55 years old.

Norman John in 2005, aged 80 years. Norman John is one of two surviving St Kildans at the time of publication. The other is Rachel Johnston (DAQ)

Neil Gillies (right) and Ewen MacDonald (left) (LM)

The Rev. Donald John Gillies (DAQ)

Neil, b. 1897, had a bad fall on his way to school when he was only ten years old and had to go to hospital in Glasgow. News came back to St Kilda that he was too ill to undergo an operation. Eventually one was carried out and, although lame throughout his life, he was able to work as a ship's wheelwright in Glasgow and died in 1990 aged 93 years.

Donald John, b. 1901, died aged 92 in 1993. He left St Kilda in 1924, moved to Glasgow and was hired by the Clyde Trust Company and assigned as a deckhand on a dredger on the river Clyde. After one year he entered the Bible Training College on Bothwell Street in Glasgow and in 1927 was appointed to the Presbyterian Church at Cape Breton in Canada. He became an Army Chaplain from 1942 to 1946, attached to the Pictou Highlanders, before landing with the Canadian Forces in Germany. After the war he was too restless to settle in a parish and eventually worked as a Chaplain in the Prison Service in Canada for over 20 years. He kept in close contact with St Kilda and preached at the service on the occasion of the 50th Anniversary of the evacuation.

He was related to Rachel MacCrimmon, who died in 1914 aged 81. She had refused to move into one of the 1860 houses, convinced that the old black-house was better adapted to life on the island. The Rev. Donald John described what her house was like: *'Inside was a stall for the cow and nearby a stall for the sheep, hens sheltered in the same area. The house was something desperate. She had a bed in the wall, a mattress of the chaff of the oats – the old fashioned way!'* Her relative, Euphemia MacCrimmon, was the last of the sennachie – the verbal historians. She died in 1869 aged 88 years.

I first met the Rev. Donald John at a St Kilda Club meeting in Edinburgh and corresponded with him several times. I was very surprised to get a telephone call from him speaking from Barrow in Furness, *'Could I come over and speak to you about St Kilda?'* I was delighted – we had a three hour 'chat' in which he never stopped talking. Fortunately, I asked him if I might record the conversation as I couldn't write notes fast enough. He kindly agreed. He was aged 86 years at the time and had an extremely strong voice. *'Surely, the St Kildans were a neglected people!'* he boomed out just before he left.

Donald Ewen, b. 1902, died on St Kilda in 1928 having caught TB in Glasgow.

Fig. 15. Resting Fulmars

House No. 16 – Donald MacDonald and Family (see 1886 Parliament photograph)

Barrington with his two St Kildan climbers – Donald MacDonald (right) with
Donald MacQueen (left) (AB)

Donald MacDonald, Lachlan's father, was chosen by Barrington to help him in his attempt to be the first non-St Kildan to climb Stac Biorach, the 240ft steeple-shaped spire of rock in Soay Sound in 1883. Barrington states:

It was Donald MacDonald who jumped from the bow of the boat on to the slimy seaweed at the foot of Stac Biorrach and went up like a cat about 50–60ft with a horse-hair rope around. I then followed with the assistance of the rope hand over hand. M'Quien came next, and all three stood on a knob (overhanging) about 18 inches square. Then followed the real crux; to go edge-ways along a ledge four inches wide with feet dangling in the air, the ledges wet with guillemot's droppings. It was terrible work, and I knew I would slip, as my fingers had not the tremendous grip of MacDonald's, who got over with an effort. I did slip, and but for the sudden powerful jerk of the horse-hair rope given by M'Quien, which rose me fully three feet and gave me a new hold, I would not be here to write this.

Barrington tells us that no sooner had he reached the top, than he began to concentrate on the even more terrifying problem of how he was to get down! Barrington considered this to have been the most dangerous climb he ever undertook although he had been to the top of most of the Alpine peaks.

Donald MacDonald was also chosen to represent the St Kildans to the Napier Commission of Enquiry in June 1883, which was a six man Royal Commission instructed to enquire into '*The condition of the crofters and cottars in the Highlands and Islands of Scotland.*'

He was to lose his life in the terrible drowning off the island of Dun in 1909, together with the two MacQueen brothers.

Stacs in Soay Sound, left Stac Biorrach, right Soay Stac. Painting by David Quine

Rachel MacDonald (Donald's wife)
with her son Angus (LM)

The photo outside No. 16 shows, to the right, Rachel MacDonald (née MacKinnon; married Donald in 1887) and their son Angus, with two visitors – the St Kildans wouldn't have hats like that! Rachel is knitting, but usually did more spinning as she suffered from bad arthritis. Angus was born in 1892 and left St Kilda after the war in 1919 or 20, in Alex Ferguson's boat carrying two tons of dried fish which he was selling for the St Kildans in exchange for provisions. Angus lived in Old Kirkpatrick and worked in the Napier and Millers Shipyard. He married Alice MacDonald, who was not a St Kildan, and had a son Donald Ian. Angus died in 1980.

The cross in the wall of House 16
(© National Trust for Scotland)

Lachlan MacDonald, 1906–1991. Here sheep shearing in 1927 on St Kilda (C)

Back row: Donald Ewen MacKinnon and Lachlan MacDonald.

Front row: Donald Gillies, Norman MacQueen and Donald MacDonald.

Lachlan MacDonald had a wonderful visual memory and a great sense of humour – a great raconteur. It was great to hear his St Kilda pronunciation of the place names. Here are a few:

Place names	*Lachlan's pronunciation*
Bearradh na cloiche moire	Beren-a quasha mora
Bearradh na h-Eige	Beren-ee-haykee (Ridge or cliff of the gap)
Boreray	Boyra
Cambir	Han Cambelyer
Below the Cambir	Soosh-shla
Dun	Doon
Gob na h-Airde	Gob na Hartcher
Geo	Gayo (hard 'g')
Rubha an Uisge	Roo Nischa
Oiseval	Oysheval
Soay	Soa
Tigh an t-sithiche	Toy na she-ish (Earth House – House of the fairies)
Tobar Gille Chille	Tobar Ille Heelee
Tobar nam Buadh	Tobar na Moor (Well of Virtues in the Great Glen)
Clagan na Rusgachan (Boreray)	Quakan a Rush-cha-han

Birds

Gannet	Sular
Guillemot	Warmi
Puffin	A Bujilla

Fig. 16. West face of Boreray

Fig. 17. Well of Virtues

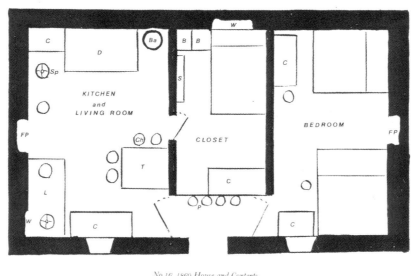

No.16, 1860 House and Contents.

Ba. Barrel of fulmars	L. Loom when in use	C. Chest for clothes	Sp. Spinning Wheel
B. Box for oatmeal	P. Pails for water	D. Dresser	T. Table
Ch. Chair	S. Shelves	FP. Fire Place	W. Wall Cupboards (D.A.Q.)

Sketch plan – inside Lachlan's house, No. 16 (DAQ)

Lachlan described going for Shearwaters:

In my day the shearwater would be the first to come on land on the main island on Carn Mor in March or the beginning of April. It was great. A queer noise they make – a lovely musical sound. They would be coming in fresh and it was a nice bird to eat and the eggs, but they were awful difficult to reach – they get amongst the rocks deep underground. There would be some coming and some going; If you were lucky to get one that was coming in he was nice and fat, but if you got one that was going away he would be lean, he would have been there for two or three days – he wasn't fed. It's a nice bird, too, and its great to hear them singing – both below you in the ground and above you.

Landing on Soay was difficult, it was very steep. You had an old pair of socks that you put on and you would jump onto the rocks – you would grip better if you had socks on. And then, once you got the rest of the party off the boats you were away, scrambling away up (about 800ft). You were roped between you until you were clear of the bad place. You would be chasing the sheep, but sometimes you couldn't do that, it was steep, you had to try to put them into a rock where there was an end where they couldn't jump away You would try to get a fat one – you wouldn't look at a wee lean one – you would leave them! You would tie them by their legs, put them on your back and carry them. The Soay sheep were wild. You would tie the four legs and you would put the head between your oxters and the feet up in the air and a rope to hold them. Sometimes you have two live sheep tied, one on your back with the legs tied, and one on your front, and a rope over your shoulders. In places where it was steep some folk would put their heads up to their legs and make a kind of bundle and you would have one arm free, or maybe two if you were in a bad place. It was kind of tricky! You didn't have much time to admire the view! The sheep were taken home, killed and we had to salt that meat for the winter.

Ewen was Donald and Rachel's first son, born in 1888. He remained a bachelor, staying on St Kilda until the evacuation when he moved to Lochaline and Savary, working for the Forestry Commission. Sadly his foot became infected, from which he died when he was only 49 years old. Williamena Barclay arrived in 1928 and stayed until the evacuation. She and the missionary, Dugald Monro, wrote to the Government and the people signed the petition expressing their desire to leave the island. Understandably, the older ones felt that they would rather stay on Hirta as the time for their departure came near. Lachlan MacDonald felt it was '*God's blessing*' that they were going as all the hard work was left to the few young men who stayed on the island and covered for the elderly and the widows.

Ewen MacDonald and Nurse Barclay (LM)

Lachlan had called on his sister Cathie in the morning and left his boots at her house when he went off for the day's work. Here, in the evening, Cathie has come to return them. She married Neil Gillies in 1917 and had the two boys Donald and Ewen. Her husband took ill and was taken to Oban hospital where he died in 1928. Cathie died in 1983 in Savary.

Donald was born in 1895 and left St Kilda in 1920 when he went to Stornoway and then on to Glasgow. He became a lay preacher and missionary to the Outer Isles – Colonsay, Manish on Harris, Callanish in Lewis. He retired to Harris. He always preached in Gaelic.

Rachel was born in 1899 and died on St Kilda, possibly of meningitis, aged 22 in 1921.

Cathie MacDonald with Lachlan's boots (LM)

St Kildans on the sheep fanks (LM)

The men have a break from their work, sitting on the huge boulders which make up the sheep fanks on An Lag. Within the outer wall the individual enclosures were owned by single or groups of families and latterly were used to keep ewes with weak lambs to give them a better start in life.

Left to right: Finlay MacKinnon, Donald Hugh MacKinnon, Neil Gillies, Lachlan MacDonald.

Fig. 18. Lichen covered gravestones

Lachlan MacDonald on the whale's tail (LM)

Lachlan's brother Angus was back on the island on holiday when they decided to go out in their boat to examine one of the whales attached to a mooring buoy in Village Bay. The photo shows Lachlan standing on a whale's tail, one brought in by the Norwegian whaling company. The boat in the foreground gives the scale – it is 22 ft long. The whalers would go out well beyond St Kilda and return with one or two whales and tie them up to the buoy in the bay, after two or three days they blew up like a balloon – if they burst the smell was absolutely awful. The boats would go out returning again and often they took away as many as six whales back to Tarbert in Harris.

In 1927 Lachlan visited Angus in Glasgow. He had a son on the coast, whom they visited in Helensburgh and Lachlan saw the possibilities of a different and wonderful way of life. Having been out in a boat, Lachlan became quite restless and was quite keen to come off St Kilda.

The Evacuation

The evacuation; Dunara Castle *(left) and the* Harebell *(MAA)*

The 1,200 sheep had to be rounded up; shepherds were brought in with their dogs but it was a difficult job as the St Kilda sheep were not managed in that way and ran round wild. They were eventually brought down to the crofts and the manse where they were fenced in and kept until the boats took them off to the auction mart in Oban.

The *Dunara Castle* took the livestock, of which ten cows had to swim out to the boat; four calves plus the sheep and the shepherds were taken to Oban. The *Harebell*, the fishery cruiser, took the people and all their belongings, mostly to Lochaline.

Lachlan MacDonald at the evacuation
on the Harebell *(LM)*

Wondering where I was coming to and how things were going to be. It turned out no too bad anyhow. It was a good day with a smooth crossing, then we came into the Sound of Mull – but we had to be shifted into a smaller boat, the Princess Louise to come into Lochaline pier. I don't suppose ever before or after was there such a crowd on Lochaline pier! Och, there was hundreds of them and the reporters and all that, and there was two taxis there at the time. We got quite a good reception. At Savary they had put the house in order and they had a fire ready for us. It turned out to be for the best.

3. AFTER THE EVACUATION

The 36 St Kildans left their island home on August 30th 1930 – most of them were provided with homes in the Lochaline district in the Sound of Mull, some went on to Oban and on to the Kincardine Estate on the Firth of Forth. Many worked with the Forestry Commission although they had never seen a tree in their lives! Life was going to be very different but the photographs help us to see how they adapted to their new circumstances.

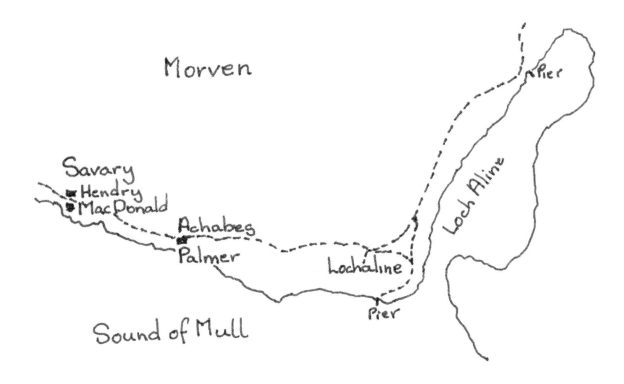

Sketch map of the Lochaline district

The map shows the locations of the homes of Ina Palmer and her three brothers at Achabeg, some 2 miles from Lochaline, and of Archie Hendry and the MacDonalds (from No. 16 St Kilda) at Savary, about 1 mile from Achabeg.

1932 – Visit of Lord Dumfries and party to St Kilda

The ownership of St Kilda had now passed over from MacLeod of MacLeod who had owned the islands until the evacuation into the hands of Lord Dumfries, who instigated this trip.

The purpose of the visit was to catch wild Soay sheep on the island of Soay and transfer them to Hirta. Other visits were made in 1933 and 1936.

Calum MacDonald, who had left the island in 1924, jumped at Alex Ferguson's invitation to join the party in 1932 and went again in 1933, staying for a month on the island lobster fishing and sea fishing – feeling much at home like the old days.

Lord Dumfries' party visiting St Kilda in June 1932 (O)

Left to right: Kate Ferguson (Alex's wife), John Gillies (father of Norman John), Christine Gillies (mother of Rachel and Cathie), possibly Lord Dumfries' brother, Finlay Gillies, Donald MacDonald, Lord Dumfries, Neil Ferguson (senior), possibly Calum MacDonald from House No. 3, possibly Calum's aunt, Annie Ferguson, Alex Ferguson, Neil Gillies (with the bad leg), one of Lord Dumfries' party, Donald Ferguson.

Lachlan MacDonald, Family and activities near Lochaline

It was an awful change for them coming from St Kilda. Cathie's husband, Neil Gillies, had died 18 months before the evacuation, leaving her to look after the two boys, Donald, aged 12 when he left, and Ewen. '*Cathie was a very kind person, always delighted to see you. She would always give you a great welcome. She was always busy – knitting socks – she also spun the wool. She had a lovely face – a bonnie woman. Donald was more serious than Ewen. He didn't like anyone coming to interview him, nor take his photo. Ewen was a high flyer, very kind hearted and lived a good life, more sociable, he liked talking to people – he was like Lachie! Rachel had very bad arthritis and was very limited in what she could do.*' (Nancy MacDonald in 2007.)

From Savary the boys went to school and then into the Forestry. During the War Ewen went to Glasgow and Donald went to Forfar for a while and worked in building with Laird brothers. Also in the house were Lachlan and his brother Ewen.

Cathie (Lachlan's sister) and her mother, Rachel MacDonald, at Savary,
working with the spinning wheel (LM)

Donald MacDonald (Lachlan's brother), wife Mary and son Donald Iain (LM)

Donald left St Kilda in the early 1920s to go to Glasgow to train as a carpenter. He actually became a missionary to the Western Isles, working in Colonsay, Harris and Lewis. He always preached in Gaelic, and retired to Harris.

St Kilda group of children and adults (LM)

Adults from left to right: Rachel (née Gillies) Johnston's mother; Angus MacDonald (Lachlan's brother); Rachel MacKinnon (died of TB), sister of Christine and Mary; Finlay MacKinnon, Forestry School, Huntly (died of TB); Annie MacKinnon, daughter of Finlay Gillies, mother of 8 from House No. 1, St Kilda, wife of Norman.

The old car with Donald Iain MacDonald (LM)

Donald Iain sitting in the old light blue Austin which Lachie and his neighbour, Archie Hendry, bought for £5. The great thing about it was that you could get up to six people in it to go to a dance!

Ewen MacDonald on horseback at Savary (LM)

Ewen didn't marry; he lived at home with his brother Donald, and mother Cathie; also with Lachlan and his brother Ewen and mother Rachel MacDonald.

Carding and spinning at Savary (LM)

On holiday Alice and Angus MacDonald are sitting outside the MacDonald's home, together with their son Donald Ian.

Haymaking at Savary (LM)

Standing: Ewen Macdonald, Mr Dean (foreman), Archie Hendry (neighbour), Unknown, Lachlan MacDonald.

Front: Duncan Sinclair (forestry), Flora MacDonald (née MacArthur), Donald Gillies (Lachlan's nephew). Flora's father was Missionary on St Kilda from 1912 to 1914, then went to Tiree.

Forestry workers (LM)

A group of the forestry workers pause for a break – from left to right: Head Forester, Finlay Gillies, John Gillies, Lachlan Macdonald.

Archie Hendry, next door to the MacDonalds at Savary, had heard such awful stories about these people coming off St Kilda that he later said, '*I got locks put on all the doors, I was afraid what they would take – I was frightened of them taking the very pipe oot of my mooth!*' But the St Kilda doors were always left open – Archie soon took the locks off his doors. He had also heard that the St Kildans never walked – they always ran! The Hendrys became great friends and were splendid neighbours.

Forestry nurseries at Morven (LM)

Ewen (left) and Lachlan MacDonald, who spent several seasons tending the young trees which had been brought on a lorry, planting them, then hoeing between the rows in the nurseries and later planting them out in their permanent positions.

Lachlan MacDonald in the Home Guard (LM)

During the Second World War Lachlan volunteered to join the Home Guard and here he is in his uniform. He regretted that he was unpaid. However, a little later he joined the Royal Observer Corps for Savary and for this he was paid and was delighted to be a despatch rider and have his own motor-bike.

Lachlan MacDonald gives a lesson to Annie Hendry (LM)

Lachlan had never seen a bicycle until he was off St Kilda for a few days in 1927 when he called at Tobermory. He commented:

I was not bothered by trams, trains and cars – we had seen pictures of them. The thing that frightened me out of my life was this fellow on a bicycle. When we pulled up at Tobermory I was standing on the quay when this fellow comes down the hill and suddenly turned off the road and onto the quay – he suddenly stops – just by me! I couldn't understand how he was able to stand upright on two wheels! When I came to ride a bicycle I found it took me weeks to learn. I couldn't get over that fellow on his bicycle! It was Annie Hendry the shepherd's daughter next door who taught me to ride, she had her own bike. In the photograph I am teaching her to spin, something she had never learnt, it was rather unusual for a man but was a skill I had learnt due to my mother's arthritis. This was also the reason for becoming a good cook – not just puffin soup!

Lachlan was delighted to move up from a bicycle to a motor-bike and later a car!

Lachlan's new car (LM)

Lachlan on horseback (LM)

Lachlan bought this Morris from near Glasgow in about 1949. It had an electric pump which would often stick, so he had to get out and under the car to give it a good knock. Lachlan had never sat a driving test but was called upon to drive the forestry workers to their site of work. He often said to himself, '*If only you fellows knew who was driving this van…!*'

The stables for the horses used by the forestry workers were in Savary, but big Hugh who was from the island of Muck and in charge of the horses lived in Lochaline. At the weekends Lachlan would save him a three mile walk back home by riding the horse back to the stables. He would also feed the horse, exercise it and generally look after it for the weekend.

Lachlan MacDonald – the hunter! (LM)

Lachlan had a great sense of humour and here he is seen having borrowed the hat, the gun and the red deer stag's head!

*How Lachlan MacDonald met Nancy Cameron –
here on her bike! (LM)*

After the evacuation Lachlan was living at Savary near Lochaline on the Sound of Mull. Nancy Cameron came from Glasgow and I wondered how they could possibly have met. Nancy told me the story. Nancy was aged about 12 years old at this time and she would come to stay in the summer holidays with her mother's cousin, Ina Palmer, who was not married and lived with her three unmarried brothers in Achabeg, only one mile away from Savary. The three brothers were shepherds; Jimmy was the head shepherd working on the Ardtornish Estate which was later taken over by the Forestry Commission. Nancy had her own bike at this time which enabled her to get around easily.

Ina Palmer and her three brothers (LM)

In the photo, from left to right, are Jimmy the head shepherd, Alec with the leggings, Ina and Ralph. They were all awfully good at the work in the house with the cleaning and washing while Ina did all the cooking. One of them was often working away and one had a bad heart and had to take special care.

At the busiest times, during dipping and clipping, they all came home for lunch and Lachlan, who was 24 by now, would often help them out. They would bring back the odd sheep to contribute to the meal.

Within a few months of August 1930 Nancy and her sister Isabel got to know the lads down the road and friendships quickly developed. Contact during the war was limited as Nancy worked for Coates in Glasgow, the firm which made threads of silks and cotton and was badly hit by the bombing. *'We worked long hours and at week-ends. We lived then just across from the Clyde and of course the Germans were desperate to bomb the yards and everything on the Clyde. On the Paisley Road there was a tramcar bombed that night – the night of the Clyde blitz. I think it was the worst night of all.* (Nancy, 2007.)

Donald, Lachlan's nephew (Cathie Gillies' son) later married Nancy's sister Isabel in 1952, they then moved to Larachbeg, near Lochaline.

Wedding of Lachlan MacDonald and Nancy Cameron, 1955 (LM)

The wedding took place in Glasgow in 1955, the service being taken by the Rev. John MacKay who came from Carloway in Lewis. The honeymoon was in Dunoon. In the 1920s John MacKay had visited St Kilda in the summer to take the services. Lachlan recalled an incident which happened when he was in his teens and had been asked to show him the Well of Virtues, so off they went to Glean Mor. Lachlan was very impressed because he was given half a crown for his labours – which was a lot of money in those days.

1980 – 50th Anniversary of the Evacuation

Lachlan was joined by his wife Nancy to be present at the service held on Hirta commemorating the 50 years since the evacuation. It had been a long journey for them, first by car from Fort William to Ullapool, then the ferry to Stornoway where they picked up the Fishery Protection vessel which brought them into Village Bay, St Kilda in the early morning. They were delighted to be back on the island and in the morning had the freedom to explore, visiting Lachlan's old house, No. 16 Main Street and many of his favourite old haunts. They met two of the soldiers outside his own house and they said they could get them a lift in a Land-rover to the top of Mullach Mor. This was a tremendous help. The Anniversary service was held in the afternoon. They just had one night on St Kilda, the men slept on the boat and the women in one of the cottages as it was unsuitable on board for them.

Lachlan and Nancy MacDonald on St Kilda in 1980 (LM)

Anniversary service on St Kilda (LM)

The St Kildans were very well represented at the service on St Kilda in 1980 to commemorate 50 years since the evacuation. The Rev. Donald John Gillies gave the address.

Left to right: Norman John Gillies, Lachlan MacDonald, Morag and May MacDonald (left in 1924), Rev. Donald John Gillies, Cathie Gillies (Oban).

Front: Rachel Johnston (née Gillies), Flora Craig (née Gillies).

My wife and I keep in touch with Nancy in Fort William – she is as bright as a button – still extremely alert about anything to do with St Kilda. She has a wonderfully clear memory and reminded us how she came to know so many of the St Kildans who had moved to the Lochaline area after the evacuation in 1930.

These photographs shed more light on the everyday life of the St Kildans, both on the island and their continued adaptability to life after the evacuation.

Fig. 19. Approaching Boreray and Stac an Armin

Selected Bibliography

Barrington, R., 1913, *Alpine Journal*

Cameron, Mary, 1973, *Our Childhood Days on St Kilda*

Carmichael, Alexander, 1865, *Carmina Gadelica*. Oliver and Boyd, Edinburgh and London

Connell, R., 1887, *St Kilda and the St Kildians*. Hamilton Adams and Co., London

Heathcote, Norman, 1900, *St Kilda*. Longmans, Green and Co.

MacGregor, Alistair Alpin, 1931, *A Last Voyage to St Kilda*. Cassell and Co.

Macgregor, D. R., 1960, The Island of St Kilda – a survey of its character and occupance, *Scot. Studies* 4

MacKenzie, Rev. J. B., 1904, Antiquities and old customs in St Kilda, compiled from notes made by the Rev. Neil MacKenzie, Minister of St Kilda, 1829–43. *Proc. Soc. Antiq. Scot.* 38, pp. 397–402; 1911, Episode in the life of the Rev. Neil MacKenzie at St Kilda from 1829–43

Quine, D. A., 1982, *St Kilda Revisited*. Privately Printed

Quine, D. A., 1988, *St Kilda Portraits*. Privately Printed

Quine, D. A., 1995 (revised 2000), *St Kilda* in *Island Guides*. Colin Baxter

Robson, M., 2005, *St Kilda – Church, Visitors and 'Natives'*. Islands Book Trust

Wilson, Dr J., 1842, *A Voyage round the Coasts of Scotland and the Isles*. Adam and Charles Black, Edinburgh